THE PARENT AND CHILD · PROGRAM ·

Starting to
Read and Write 1

Jane Salt

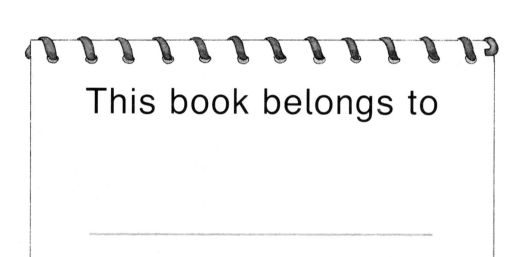

This book belongs to

Illustrated by June Goulding

To Parents

When your child goes to school there are many concepts and skills she or he will start learning before beginning to read. This book helps develop the special ways of looking, listening, predicting and remembering that children need to become readers. It also provides plenty of opportunities for talking together. Talking about the stories, pictures and activities is very valuable, because it is through talk at this stage that children develop their use and knowledge of language.

Here are some ways you can help with the first steps in reading when you read this book with your child.

Make sure your child understands

1. The correct way to hold a book, by asking your child to open the book for you.

2. How the pages turn, by demonstrating and then asking your child to do it for you.

3. Which way the print goes, by following it from left to right with your finger. When the text is very simple (e.g. Humpty Dumpty sat on the wall, Tim is little) your child may be able to follow the words, too.

    Remember to lift your finger off the page at the end of a line and carry it over to the start of the new line.

4. How each word you speak is a separate group of letters by pointing out interesting or recurring words. Point out the difference between long and short words.

Always make sure that your child has plenty of time to discuss the pictures. Encourage the child to guess what the words say from the picture. Do not forget the value of repetition! Young children love it, and where the text is simple, a child may learn it by heart and "read" it while pointing to the words. This is the beginning of being able to read. If you think your child needs more practice, you could return to the first book in this series; children enjoy repeating activities with which they're familiar.

Always give your child as much help as is needed and lots of praise for the smallest achievement. For most children, two or three pages at a time will be enough. Make sure you stop before your child loses interest.

Two games are included in this book because games are of particular value in learning. The games in this book practice letter sound recognition and matching skills.

The most important way you can help your child to read is by showing that reading is fun!

This is Humpty Dumpty.

Can you find him in the picture below?

Humpty Dumpty is on the shelf.

3

Humpty Dumpty sat on a wall.

Humpty Dumpty had a great fall.

4

All the King's horses and all the King's men,

Couldn't put Humpty together again.

Can you find a path to Humpty Dumpty?

Start here.
Then trace the path to him with your finger.

Finish coloring the Humpty Dumpties so that they match their partners.

How many Humpty Dumpties are there on this page?

Tim and Liz

Liz is big.

Tim is little.

But Mom is biggest.

Tim's bike is little.

Liz's bike is big.

But Mom's bike is the biggest.

9

This is Tim and Liz's bedroom.

Can you see Liz's shoes?
Can you see Tim's hat?
Which is Tim's bed?

Draw a path for Tim down the middle of each road.

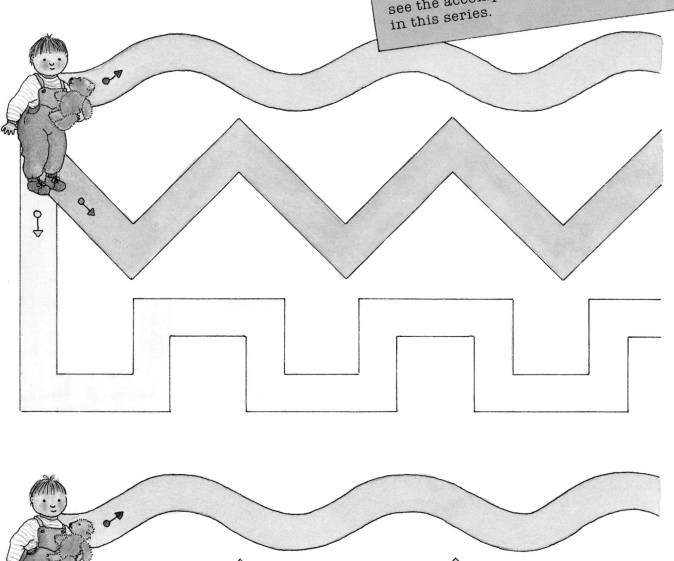

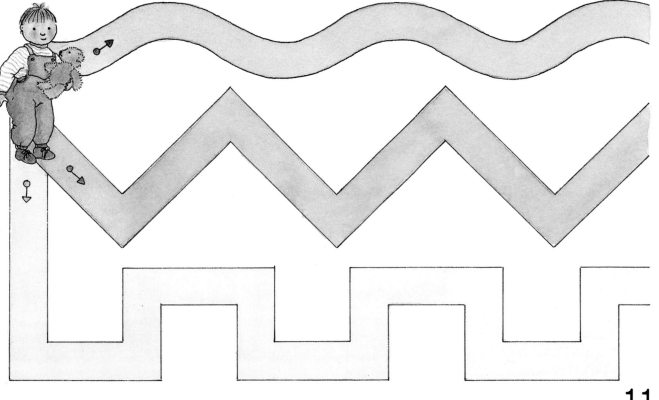

11

We built a tent in our backyard.

Karen's kittens

Karen has lots of kittens.
Can you see what they are all
doing in the picture?

How many kittens are there?
What do you think will happen next?
Turn the page to find out.

Note to Parents

Discuss the picture before reading the text with your child. On a second reading, your child may be able to guess the end of the sentences.
Remember to point to the words.

The black kitten has spilled the milk.
The white kitten has fallen into the bucket.
The ginger kitten has eaten the chicken.
The striped kitten has knocked over the shopping.
The black and white kitten has pulled
down the curtain.
Poor Karen! What a mess to clear up.

14

Karen is knitting a blanket for the kittens' basket. Can you finish the pattern?

Note to Parents
Help your child trace over the patterns and the dots with a finger before coloring them.

Tig and Tag

These two puppies are sisters.
They look the same, don't they?
Do you think you can tell them apart?

Tig has a big black spot on her head. She has a little black nose.

Tag has a little black spot on her head. She has a pink nose.

Note to Parents

Can your child notice any other differences?
What are the similarities?

Spread the cards face down on a table. Take turns choosing a card. If the card has the same color background as your castle, put it in the right place and take another turn. If not, it is the other person's turn. To win you must fill your castle first.

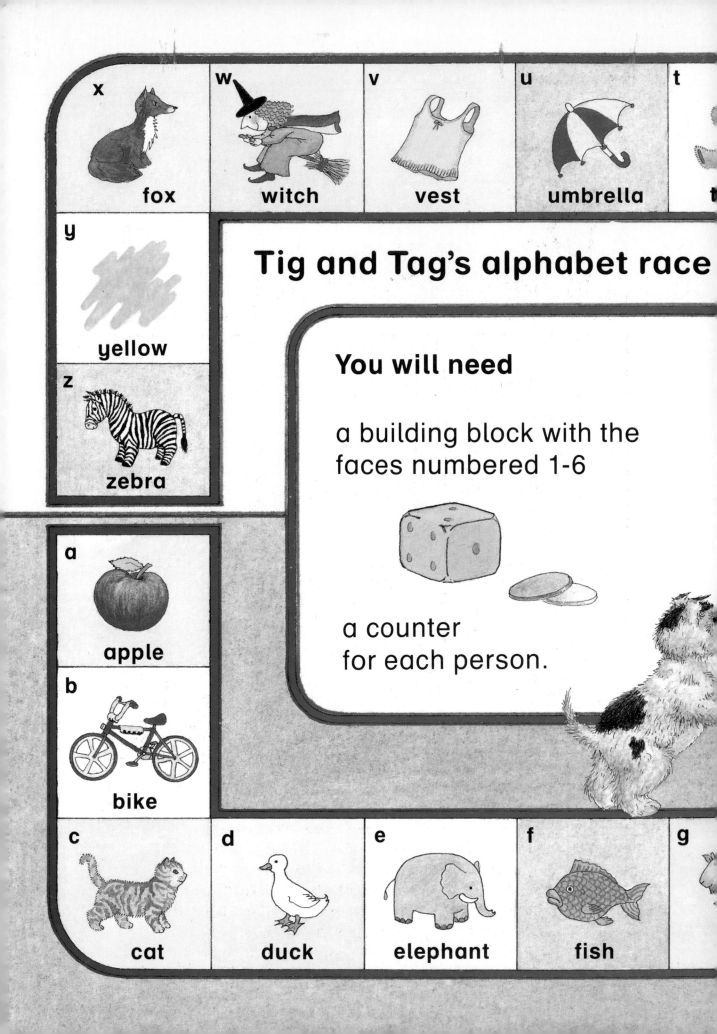

x fox

w witch

v vest

u umbrella

t t

y yellow

z zebra

Tig and Tag's alphabet race

You will need

a building block with the faces numbered 1-6

a counter for each person.

a apple

b bike

c cat

d duck

e elephant

f fish

g

s seal

r rabbit

q queen

p puppy

o orange

n nest

m monkey

l lion

How to play

Take turns tossing the block.

Move forward the number of squares shown on the block.

Say the word on the square you land on.

The first person to get to **z** wins.

h hat

i igloo

j jewel

k king

Castle Game

A game for 2 players.
Cut out the pictures on page 31 and glue them on cards.
Choose a castle. One of you be red, the other blue.

Is this Tig?
No.
It's Tag hiding
under a chair.

Is this Tig?
Yes.
It's Tig chewing the rug.

17

Here are some other brothers and sisters.

Can you spot the differences
in the pictures?

Kit and Kim kitten.

Minnie and Molly Monkey.

Note to Parents

Can your child hear the same sound repeated in the names e.g. **T**ilak, **T**arlok **T**iger?

Gina and Gerry Giraffe.

Tilak and Tarlok Tiger.

Dinah Dragon tries to help

Note to Parents

This is a story for you to read.
Your child may like to join in with
the words in the speech bubbles an
the repetitive parts of the story.

"What a lot of bad tempered dragons," said Dinah Dragon. "How can I stop them all from quarreling?"

Now Dinah was a magic dragon, so she sat down to think of a spell.

"I know," she said, "red's a happy color. I'll turn everything in Dragon Land red."

So Dinah Dragon twirled and she swirled and twitched her tail, and everything turned red.

"Oh no!" moaned Dan Dragon. "I don't like this. It's like living in a tomato."

So Dinah Dragon twirled and she swirled and twitched her tail, and everything turned blue.

"Help!" cried Debbie Dragon. "I don't like this. It's like living at the bottom of the sea."

So Dinah Dragon twirled and she swirled and twitched her tail, and everything turned yellow.

"Horrible!" shouted Dora Dragon. "I don't like this. It's like living in a bowl of custard."

"Oh dear! Oh dear! I really don't know what to do next," sighed Dinah Dragon. "Can you help me?"

Note to Parents

Can your child help Dinah think of what to do next? Discuss ideas and then write them for your child in the space provided. You can use extra sheets if the story gets really long!

Here are some dragons for you to color.

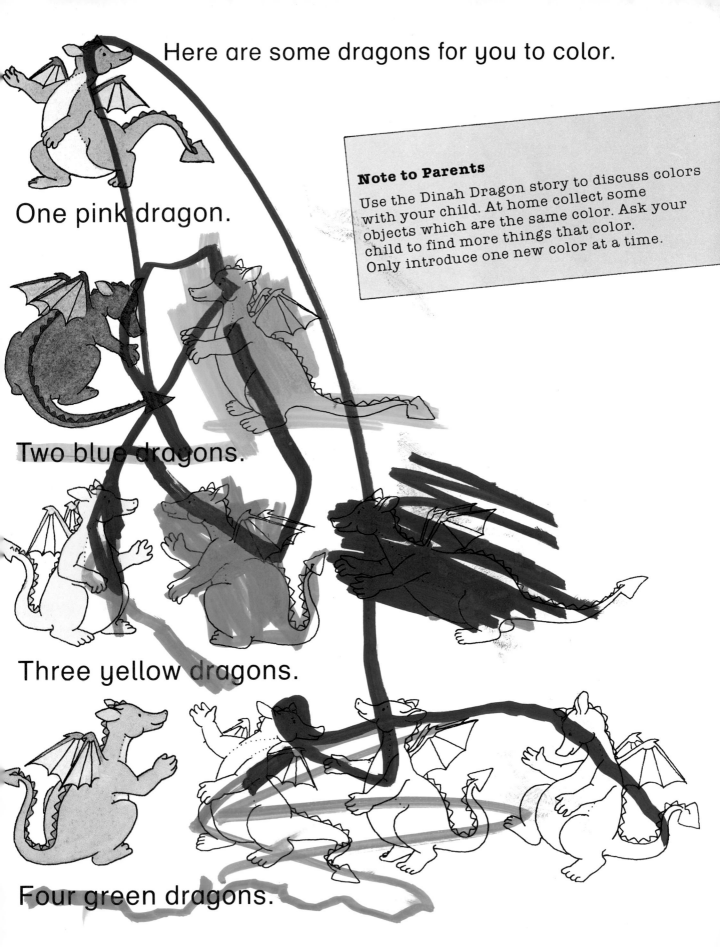

One pink dragon.

Note to Parents

Use the Dinah Dragon story to discuss colors with your child. At home collect some objects which are the same color. Ask your child to find more things that color. Only introduce one new color at a time.

Two blue dragons.

Three yellow dragons.

Four green dragons.

How many dragons are there all together?

23

What happens next?

Take a guess.

Then look on the next page and find the right picture.

Note to Parents

Help the child describe what is happening in the pictures.

Think up names.

The knight is called _____.

The witch is called _____.

The princess is called _____.

How many things beginning with **p** can you find in this picture?

Did you find these?

princess   prince   picture   purse

What is the same about these words?

table   tree   tiger   teddy bear

They all begin with **t**.

Can you think of any
more words beginning with **t**?

Note to Parents

Help your child trace
over the letters **p** and **t**
to learn their shape.
For practice with
writing letters see the
accompanying
workbooks in the series.

Finger puppets

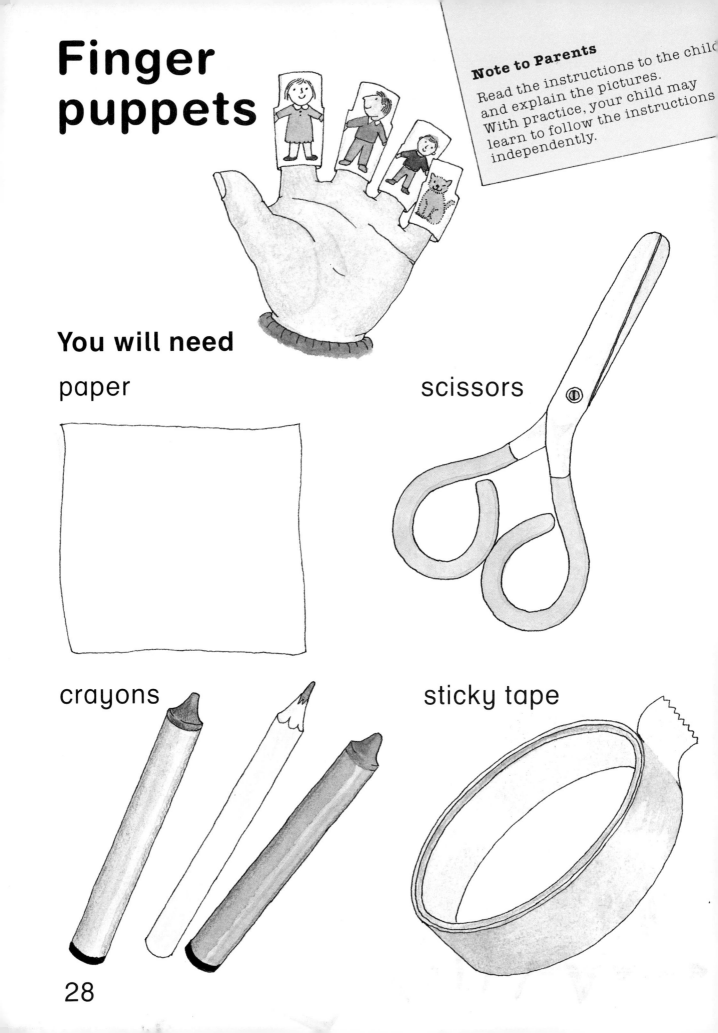

You will need

paper

scissors

crayons

sticky tape

28

How to make the puppet

Cut a piece of paper
this size.

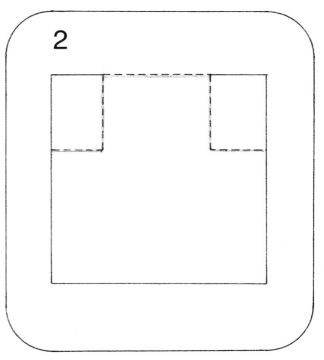

Draw a shape like this
on the paper. Cut it out.

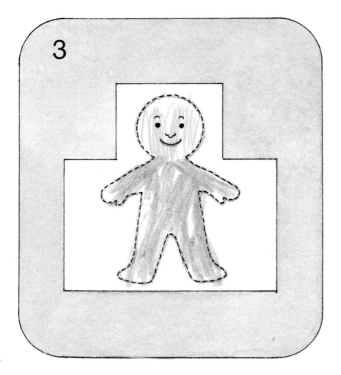

Draw your puppet in the
middle of the paper.

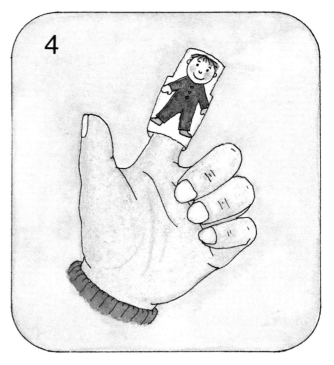

Fold it around your finger.
Tape it together.

You can make lots of different finger puppets.

Can you name these puppets?

Good-bye!

The pictures on this page are for use in the Castle Game in the center of the book.

**This page has been left blank
to allow for the cutting activity
on the previous page.**